Animal Lives
LIONS
Sally Morgan

QED Publishing

Written by Sally Morgan
Designed by Q2A Solutions
Editor Tom Jackson
Map by PCGraphics (UK) Ltd

Publisher Steve Evans
Creative Director Louise Morley
Editorial Manager Jean Coppendale

Printed and bound in China

Picture Credits

Getty: Front cover, Gail Shumway 5, Jonathan
and Angela 15, Paul Souders 19, Art Wolfe 27,
Joseph Van Os 25, 30, Andy Rouse 1, 30
Corbis: Paul A. Souders 4, Theo Allofs 7,
Joe McDonald 8-9, 10, Alissa Crandall 12,
Mary Ann McDonald 15, Tom Brakefield 26
Stillpictures: Martin Harvey 17, 19, 21, 23
(BIOS), 25, 28-29, Michael Fairchild 11,
N. Granier 13, BIOS 30
Ecoscene: Fritz Polking 17, Karl Ammann 29
FLPA: Fritz Polking 21, Mandal Ranjit 7,
MITSUAKI IWAGO/Minden Pictures 23

Words in **bold** are
explained in the
Glossary on page 31.

Contents

The lion 4

Lion types 6

Where do lions live? 8

Living in a pride 10

Beginning life 12

Growing up 14

Predators 16

Lion senses 18

Lion movement 20

Hunting 22

Living in a territory 24

Communication 26

Lions under threat 28

Life cycle 30

Glossary 31

Index 32

The lion

The lion is often called 'King of the Beasts' because of its great strength. It is a big cat and is related to tigers, cheetahs and leopards. All these cats are skilful hunters that eat meat.

Lion fact

Male lions weigh about 200kg and lionesses weigh about 150kg.

4

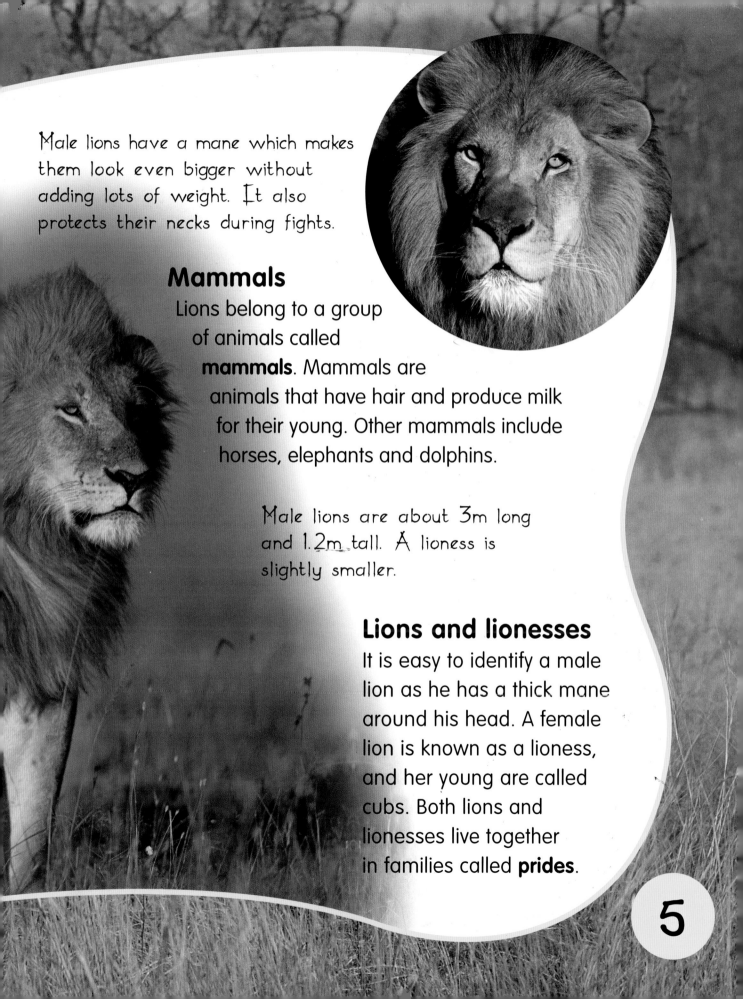

Male lions have a mane which makes them look even bigger without adding lots of weight. It also protects their necks during fights.

Mammals

Lions belong to a group of animals called **mammals**. Mammals are animals that have hair and produce milk for their young. Other mammals include horses, elephants and dolphins.

Male lions are about 3m long and 1.2m tall. A lioness is slightly smaller.

Lions and lionesses

It is easy to identify a male lion as he has a thick mane around his head. A female lion is known as a lioness, and her young are called cubs. Both lions and lionesses live together in families called **prides**.

5

Lion types

There is only one species, or type, of lion. However, there are slight variations between lions living in different parts of the world, so this species is divided into five groups called subspecies. They are the Angolan, Asiatic, Masai, Senegalese and Transvaal lions.

The Asiatic lion has a shorter mane and a thicker coat than the African lion.

Asiatic lions

All of the subspecies live in Africa except the Asiatic lions. Asiatic lions are very rare, living in just one forest in India.

There are several differences between the Asiatic lion and the African lion. The Asiatic lion has a longer tassel on its tail and a tuft of hair on its elbows.

Male lions in Africa have a thick mane that stretches down their back.

Types of lion

Subspecies	Where they live
Angolan	Zimbabwe, Angola and the Congo
Asiatic	Gir Forest in India
Masai	East Africa
Senegalese	West Africa
Transvaal	South Africa

7

Where do lions live?

In the past, lions were found in many more places than they are today. They roamed across Africa, southern Europe, the Middle East and as far east as India. Now they are found only in parts of Africa and India.

All African lions live south of the Sahara Desert. The Asiatic lion is found only in the Gir Forest in north-western India.

Lion

Two thousand years ago, gladiators in Rome often fought lions in public arenas.

fact

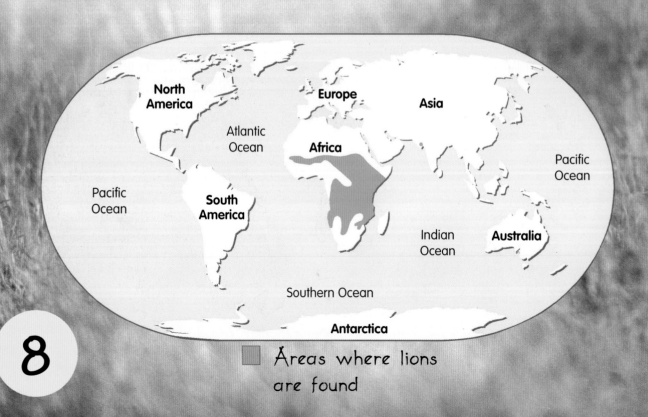

North America

Europe

Asia

Atlantic Ocean

Africa

Pacific Ocean

Pacific Ocean

South America

Indian Ocean

Australia

Southern Ocean

Antarctica

Areas where lions are found

Lion habitats

Most African lions live on the **savannah** – a flat grassland with few trees. The lions share the savannah with grazing animals such as antelopes, zebras and wildebeest. Lions kill and eat these animals. In India the lions live in a forest **habitat** and eat deer.

There are few places to hide on the savannah. A lion's yellow coat makes it hard to spot in the long, dry grass.

Living in a pride

Lion

When a male lion or group of males takes over a pride, they kill all the youngest cubs. Then they mate with the lionesses to have their own young.

fact

Lions live in groups called prides. A typical pride is made up of between four and twelve lionesses, their cubs and up to six adult males. The lionesses are all related, but none of them is related to the pride's adult males.

A pride of lions works together to look after the young and find food.

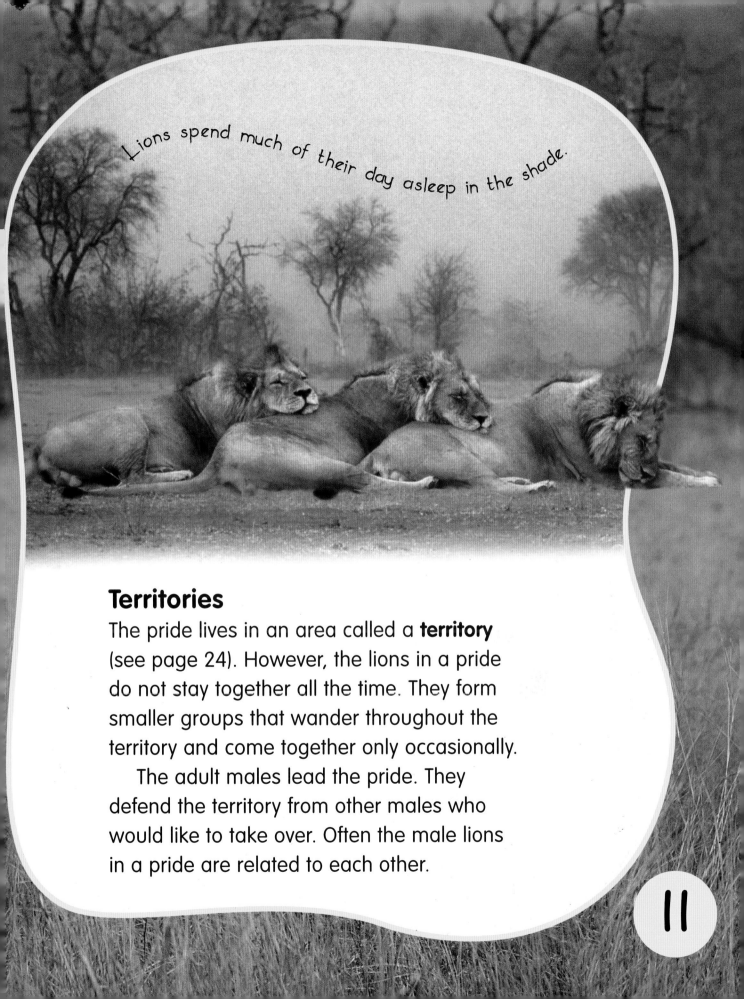

Lions spend much of their day asleep in the shade.

Territories

The pride lives in an area called a **territory** (see page 24). However, the lions in a pride do not stay together all the time. They form smaller groups that wander throughout the territory and come together only occasionally.

The adult males lead the pride. They defend the territory from other males who would like to take over. Often the male lions in a pride are related to each other.

Beginning life

After mating, the lioness is **pregnant** for about 15 weeks. The cubs are very small, weighing just 2kg when they are born. There are normally two or three cubs in a litter. The lioness feeds the cubs with her milk.

The lioness has to hide her cubs in a safe place when she goes hunting. Every few days she moves her cubs to a new hiding place, in case **predators** have spotted them.

Hungry cubs rush up to a lioness to suckle her milk.

Lion

Newborn cubs weigh just one hundredth of the weight of an adult lion. Only one in every four lion cubs survives to become an adult.

fact

This lioness is carrying her young cub to a safe hiding place.

Meeting the pride

When a cub is two months old, it is introduced to the other lions in the pride. The younger cubs are left together in a nursery group. The adult lionesses take turns to look after them.

Growing up

Lion cubs feed on their mother's milk for about six months. They grow teeth when they are three months old and begin to eat meat. When the pride kills an animal, the cubs are taken to it by their mother to practise chewing on meat.

Play fighting

Playing helps cubs to learn hunting and fighting skills. When they are one year old, the lionesses allow the cubs to follow them on a hunt. At first, the youngsters only watch, but soon they begin to take part. The youngsters also hunt for small **prey** on their own.

During play fights lion cubs learn not to hurt each other when they scratch and bite.

Lion

A lioness will give milk to her sisters' and cousins' cubs as well as her own.

fact

A lioness takes young cubs to feed after a hunt.

Stay or go?

When they become adults, lionesses stay with the pride, but the male lions are driven away once they are about three years old. Often they go off with other males of the same age and form a male-only group.

15

Predators

The lionesses do most of the hunting. They are strong enough to kill prey that is as large as they are. Their claws are long, strong and curved, and hook into the prey's flesh.

Lions cannot run fast over long distances. They have to sneak up close to their prey before dashing in for the kill.

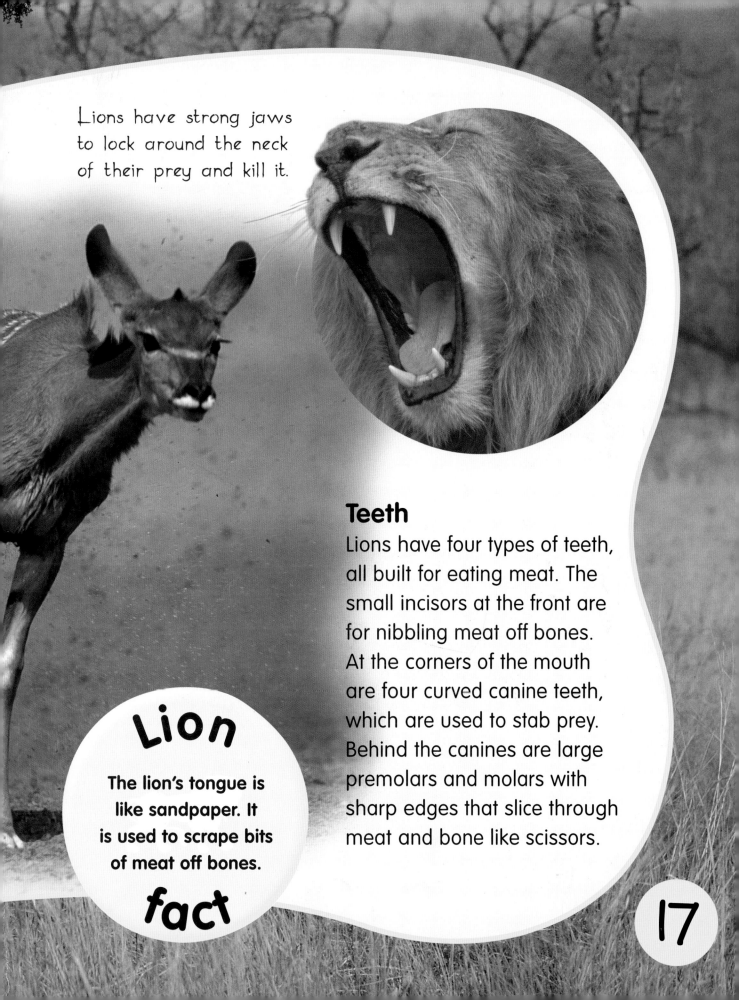

Lions have strong jaws to lock around the neck of their prey and kill it.

Teeth

Lions have four types of teeth, all built for eating meat. The small incisors at the front are for nibbling meat off bones. At the corners of the mouth are four curved canine teeth, which are used to stab prey. Behind the canines are large premolars and molars with sharp edges that slice through meat and bone like scissors.

Lion

The lion's tongue is like sandpaper. It is used to scrape bits of meat off bones.

fact

Lion senses

Lions usually hunt at dusk and at dawn, when the sun is low. The lion's prey cannot see as well in the dim light, but a lion's senses of sight, smell and hearing are perfect for hunting in the gloom.

The lion's large eyes glow in the dark, just like a pet cat's.

Excellent eyesight

A lion's eyes are the biggest of any cat. They point forwards and this helps them to judge distances well. This is especially useful when a lion is chasing and leaping onto prey. Their eyes are also very sensitive to movement. However, if an animal lies really still, the lion will probably not spot it.

Hearing

Lions turn their head in the direction of a sound in order to hear it better. Their ears can twist slightly, too, and this helps them to work out exactly where the sound is coming from.

Lions do most of their hunting in the dim light of dawn or dusk.

Lion movement

Lions are large animals but they can charge forwards at speeds of 50 kilometres an hour for a short distance. They can also leap 9 metres – that is almost as long as a bus. A lioness can run faster than a male lion. Her body is better suited to hunting, whereas the male's heavier body is better for fighting.

Lion

Lions have five toes on their front paws and four toes on their back paws.

fact

Lions have pads under their paws which help them to creep up on their prey.

Lions run with a series of long bounds.

Silent walking

Lions can walk almost silently. Under each toe there is a pad that cushions their paws and softens any noise. Their claws can be pulled back, or retracted, inside their toes when they are not being used. This protects the claws from being worn down.

Hunting

Lionesses do hunt alone, but by working together they can kill large prey, such as zebras or buffalo. A large animal is enough to feed a pride for several days.

Lionesses creep up slowly on their prey. They are very patient and may stalk prey for hours.

Hunting together

At the start of a hunt, the lionesses spread out in a fan. Some walk towards the prey, forcing it towards the other lionesses that are hidden in the grass. These lionesses ambush the prey when it is close enough.

This pride of lions has brought down a buffalo.

Taking turns

After the prey animal has been pulled down, the lionesses kill it by biting its neck to stop it breathing. The male lions are always the first to feed. Once they have finished, the females feed, and then finally the cubs are allowed to eat.

Lion

A hungry lion eats almost anything and often scavenges for dead animals. Lions steal as much as half of their food from other predators, such as hyenas and leopards.

fact

Living in a territory

A pride of lions lives in an area called a territory. They find all their food and water within this area.

The size of the territory depends on how much food is available. If there are plenty of prey animals, the territory is small, for example about 20 square kilometres. In less crowded places, the lions can occupy as much as 400 square kilometres.

Lions can inflict serious injuries on each other when they fight.

Lion fact

Lions often share their territory with other predators, such as cheetahs and leopards.

Lions can recognize each other by the smell of their urine.

Defending their land

The male lions patrol the territory. They mark trees and boulders with their **urine**. The smell tells other lions to stay away. If they do meet lions from other prides, they will often fight each other.

Communication

At dawn and dusk, the roar of lions can be heard across the savannah. Roaring is one way that lions stay in contact with each other. Male lions roar to warn other males to stay away. Lionesses use roars to call their cubs. Other sounds made by lions include moans, grunts, snarls and growls.

Both lions and lionesses roar, but the male's roar is deeper.

Touch and feel

Body contact is very important to lions. Lions of the same pride greet each other by rubbing their cheeks together. Sometimes they rub their necks and their bodies against each other, too.

A lion's bumpy tongue works like a comb.

Grooming

During quiet parts of the day, pride members often lick each other. This is called grooming. It cleans the fur, removes ticks and fleas, and also helps lions in a pride stay friends.

Lions under threat

In the past, people went on safari in Africa to shoot wildlife, not to look at it. A few people still pay to shoot lions just for fun. For this reason, and many others, the number of lions in the wild is falling.

Lions are used to vehicles and often walk right up to them to look at the tourists inside.

Under threat

Other threats include farming and diseases. As the number of people in Africa increases, more of the savannah is used for farming. Dogs belonging to local people also spread diseases to the lions.

These scientists are fitting transmitters to two **drugged** lionesses. This will allow the scientists to follow the lions' movements.

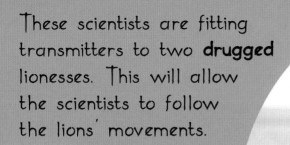

Conservation

Many areas of the African savannah are now national parks, where the wildlife is protected. Tourists visiting the parks bring money into the area, which can be used to help local people and to protect the lions.

Lion

Ten years ago there were 100 000 lions in Africa but now there are just 17 000. There are even fewer Asiatic lions. Only 200 lions are left in the protected Gir Forest.

fact

29

Life cycle

A lioness is ready to breed by the time she reaches three years old. She gives birth to a litter of two or three cubs. The lionesses stay with the pride, but the young males are chased away by the time they reach three. A lion may live for 15 years in the wild, but as many as 25 years in a zoo.

Cub

Older cub

Adult male lion

Glossary

conservation protecting wildlife from being damaged by the activities of humans

drugged knocked out or temporarily put to sleep

habitat the place where an animal or plant lives

mammal an animal that is usually covered in hair and gives birth to live young rather than laying eggs. Female mammals produce milk to feed their young

predator an animal that hunts other animals

pregnant a female animal that has a baby or babies developing inside her

prey an animal that is hunted by other animals

pride a group of lions that live together

savannah grassland in a hot country

scavenge to feed on dead and decaying bodies of animals

territory an area where a lion spends its life and where it finds all of its food

urine water that is passed out of the body of a mammal

Index

Angolan lions 6, 7
Asiatic lions 6, 7

body contact 27
breeding 30
buffalo 22, 23

cats 4, 18
cheetahs 4, 24
claws 16, 21
communication 26–7
conservation 29, 31
cubs 5, 10, 12, 13, 14, 23

diseases 28
drugged 29, 31

eyes 18, 19

farming 28
feeding 9, 14, 15, 23
fighting 5, 14, 20, 24, 25

Gir Forest 8, 29
gladiators 8
grooming 27
growing up 14–15

habitat 9, 31
hearing 18, 19

hunting 4, 14, 16–17, 18, 19, 20, 22–3

jaws 17

leaping 20
leopards 4, 23, 24
life cycle 30
life span 30
lionesses 5, 10, 12–13, 20, 22–3, 30
feeding cubs 12, 14, 15
litter 12, 30

male lions 5, 10, 11, 20, 30
killing cubs 10
leaving pride 15
mammals 5, 31
mane 5, 6, 7
Masai lions 6, 7
milk 12, 14, 15
movement 20–1

national parks 29
numbers of lions 29
nursery groups 13

paws 20, 21
playing 14
predators 12, 16–17, 31
pregnancy 12, 31
prey 14, 16–17, 18, 22, 31

pride 5, 10–11, 13, 15, 24, 27, 30, 31
roaring 26, 27
running 16, 20–1

safaris 28
savannah 9, 28, 29, 31
scavenging 23, 31
Senegalese lions 6, 7
senses 18–19
sight 18
size 4, 5
smell 18, 25
subspecies 6, 7
suckling 12

tail 6
teeth 14, 17
territory 11, 24–5, 31
threats to lions 28–9
tigers 4
toes 20, 21
tongue 17, 27
touch 27
Transvaal lions 6, 7
types of lion 6–7

urine 25, 31

walking 21
weight 4, 5, 12, 13